Social Disorganization and Strain Theories: A Historical Perspective on Contemporary Theories of Criminology

Social Disorganization and Strain Theories: A Historical Perspective on Contemporary Theories of Criminology

Patrick E. Mernick

B.A., M.A. Criminology "Magna Cum Laude"

Social Disorganization and Strain Theories: A **Historical Perspective on Contemporary Theories of Criminology**

Table of Contents

1

Social Disorganization and Strain Theories: A Historical Perspective on Contemporary Theories of Criminology

Abstract

Highlighted as significant in this paper is the impact from social disorganization and strain theory on developing new paradigms and criminological theories. An intense analysis of these early theories is required in order to conduct a critical examination of contemporary criminological philosophies. Contemporary criminologists and academic scholars continue to employ forms of social disorganization and strain theory into new theoretical models. The strengths and deficiencies attributable to this early theory continue to enhance understanding of a plethora of studies proposed as facilitators in the quest to determine causation of deviant, criminal behaviors. The emergence of new criminological theories, or "theoretical integration" as labeled by some, suggests it is problematic to assert one singular criminological theory will explain the correlation between crime rates, anticipated and actual criminal behavior, and the likelihood of continued deviant, criminal acts. A host of individual and contextual factors is clearly worthy of exploration in an attempt to understand the complexity of the nature of criminal behavior. It is significant to recognize it is impossible to conduct an analysis into contemporary application of social disorganization and strain theories without a broader comprehension of earlier theories. Key points examined in this paper will also include social disorganization theory, which draws a nexus between crime rates and characteristics that are ecological (based upon the environment) in nature and the likelihood of criminal behavior.

Social Disorganization and Strain Theories: A Historical Perspective on Contemporary Theories of Criminology

Introduction

A major focus of this paper is placed on the strengths and deficiencies of social disorganization and strain theory. Although there is a plethora of literature on these theories, one aim of this paper is to examine the revelations from a historical perspective, as well as from an analysis of the current status and application of contemporary criminological theories that have fundamental roots in earlier theory. Consequently, it is imperative an examination of the evolution of early criminological theories be conducted in order to facilitate an understanding of problematic issues that are inherent in contemporary criminological theories and to forecast potential calls for future research. New paradigms for research models are also vital in order to address the failures of earlier criminological theories as a matter of practicality and application to any given criminological problem.

There is a measurable and noticeable impact from strain and social disorganization theory on developing new paradigms and criminological theories. An intense analysis is required in order to conduct a critical examination of contemporary criminological theories, which continue to employ forms of social disorganization and strain theory into new theoretical models. The strengths and deficiencies attributable to social disorganization and strain theory continue to enhance understanding of a plethora of studies proposed as facilitators in the quest to determine causation of deviant criminal behaviors. The emergence of new criminological theories, labeled "theoretical integration" by some, suggests it is problematic to assert that one singular criminological theory will explain the correlation between crime rates, anticipated and actual criminal behavior, and the likelihood of continued deviant, criminal acts. An attempt to understand the complexity of the nature of criminal behavior should include the exploration of a

Social Disorganization and Strain Theories: A Historical Perspective on Contemporary Theories of Criminology

host of individual and contextual factors. It is significant to recognize that without a broader comprehension of earlier theories, any analysis into contemporary applications of social disorganization and strain theory will be deficient. Key points examined in this paper will highlight social disorganization theory, which draws a nexus between crime rates and characteristics that are ecological (based upon the environment) in nature and the likelihood of criminal behavior. This paper will also focus on strain and ecological theories, social control principles, Edwin Sutherland's paradigm, differential association, control theory, empirical studies, social learning schools, self-control, and the narrative, all of which have a connection with social disorganization and strain models.

General Strain Theory: Foundation, Empirical Analysis, and Contemporary Criminology

The focus of strain theory to a large extent is on negative and delinquent behavior. According to original strain theorists, rewards and achievements have no nexus with criminal behavior. Social comparison is noticeably absent from the ideologies proposed by Merton and other earlier strain theorists. Strain theory has been categorized into several different areas. One category focuses on the actual goal of the theory. A second focus illicits that strain is utilized as a vehicle of measurement which deletes strain from stimuli an also removes negative valued stimuli. It cannot be gainsaid that most contemporary criminologists including Hirschi, now opine that strain theory that includes certain variables are not instrumental in any analysis attempting to explain deviant behavior or crime.

Today, many paradigms include variables that are typically associated with other theories, such as social learning, social control, and differential theories. New paradigms, other than those first articulated by Merton, relied unnecessarily on various assumptions that did not

Social Disorganization and Strain Theories: A Historical Perspective on Contemporary Theories of Criminology

address the effect of stress in social psychology and due process. Merton, to his credit, decided to add to the initial theory the concept of including relationships that had a negative impact. Contemporary criminologists are now addressing emotions and urban underclasses. These new theorists have treated with benign neglect the connection between crime and delinquency, which earlier strain theorists stressed as causative factors. New paradigms revisiting the originally cultivated strain theory did not include observational and empirical data. Strain theorists now recognize that social control and differential association theories are different in many respects from basic strain theory, but also share some commonalities with this theory. It is poignant to note that the strain, differential association, and social control theories attempt to explain deviance and delinquent behavior by analyzing a respective individual's relationships on a social level. Regardless, strain theory initially concentrated on relationships leading to deviant behavior and what motivates delinquent behavior.

The focus of subsequent differential and social learning and control theorists is not on the negative, but rather how negativity impacts a lack of social control, which results in such things as delinquent behavior and subsequent deviant behavior or abuse. Strain theorists stress that the absence of positive value goals correlates to delinquency. The strain theories of Merton, Cohen, Cloward, and Ohlin, as well as contemporary criminologists, stress the need to include the effect of immediate goals on adolescents. Original strain theorists to a great extent ignore the distinctions in class stratifications (middle vs. lower class environments), which may have an impact on respective notions of the ability to achieve middle class goals and the inability to comprehend the value of economic success and its deterrent effect on delinquency. **Distinguishing Factors Found in Differential and Social Control Theories**

Social Disorganization and Strain Theories: A Historical Perspective on Contemporary Theories of Criminology

Strain theories, such as those initially developed by Merton, stressed negativity where people were treated unfairly based upon deviant relationships that had a negative impact. Other criminologists, such as Agnew (1985), expanded Merton's concept to incorporate those relationships that considered negative stimuli. Social control theorists stressed conventional positive relationships and environments where adolescents were prone to delinquency because of the absence of cohesive family relationships, parental failures to monitor children, and effective sanctions, to name a few. Consequently, the social learning theory differs from conventional strain theory in that it takes into account the reasons for delinquency, which include, but are not limited to, positive reinforcement of behavior, learning conventional value systems, and the fact that many children are affected by negative non-conventional relationships that are reinforced by angst, anxiety, and anger. Social learning theory also examines the effect of positive reinforcement, which according to the earlier general strain theorists is not significant to analyze deviant behavior. General strain theorists fail to consider the correlation between those acts that motivate delinquency other than attributing this behavior to the negative environment. Recent criminologists that address strain theory acknowledge the importance of analyzing the effect of the failure of adolescents to believe they can achieve success.

Immediate Goals According to Contemporary Revisionists of Strain Theory

The deficiency attributed to earlier strain theorists is that original strain adherents ignored genetics, intelligence, skills, and the effect of poor visions of success based upon the inability to understand how middle class values can deter various culturally accepted noble goals. The absence of empirical studies by the likes of Merton and other earlier adherents to general strain theory is also a noticeable deficiency that buttresses strain theory. This is because those theories

Social Disorganization and Strain Theories: A Historical Perspective on Contemporary Theories of Criminology

that lack empirical research tend to ignore variables that address goals, successful achievements, and noble expectations for success.

Other Deficiencies of Original Strain Theory

Cohen (1965) argued in a follow-up to his strain theory, the neglect of social comparison is a major shortcoming of strain theory. Goals are not entirely based on culturally based goals. Strain theory and revisionists often ignore the ideology possessed by equity theorists that presupposes that "Individuals in a relationship will compare the ratio of their outcomes and inputs to the ratio(s) of specific others in the relationship. If the ratios are equal to one another, they feel that the outcomes are fair or just" (Agnew, 1992, p. 53). Agnew (1992) also focuses on inequity because he posits that those who are not treated with equity resort to abuse, delinquency, rebellion, and insurmountable obstacles that affect achievement oriented goals. Therefore, those individuals treated inequitably may resort to taking out their anxiety on those who these individuals feel are responsible for their inability to achieve success.

Background

There are three pertinent articles published by Merton, Kubrin, and Weitzer, (2009), as well as Lowenkamp, Cullen, and Pratt (2012), which reveal various strengths and weaknesses in strain and social disorganization theory. These articles provide an initial foundation and methodology through which criminologists may conduct a thorough examination of the current application of social disorganization and strain theory. Criminologists may also use these to evaluate the merger of theories, and survival or rejection into contemporary criminological research.

Social Disorganization and Strain Theories: A Historical Perspective on Contemporary Theories of Criminology

Social disorganization theory has evolved over time. At first glance, this theory appears to be the best method (especially if it incorporates intermittent variables) to predict and correlate various ecological and other conditions with the occurrence of deviant behavior. The inclusion of intermittent variables and other condition precedents to deviant behavior has had an impact on contemporary criminological theorists, leading to reexamination of earlier research.

The frequently cited Sampson and Groves test of social organization theory, based on the British Crime Survey and data conducted in 1982, is now deemed by many criminologists and sociologists to be a classic. It expands upon social disorganization theory by suggesting an individual's residence, i.e., the neighborhood lived in, is more significant than identifiable features, such as gender, race, and age, in determining the probability an individual will engage in various illegal activities. As such street crime tends to be centralized within particular geographic locations.

Subsequently, Lowenkamp, Cullen, and Pratt (2003) addressed the replication of the Sampson and Groves test on social disorganization theory admirably. These authors attempted to determine whether their findings were an anomaly or were capable of systematic replication. The same goal posited by Lowenkamp et al. is true of the studies analyzed by Veysey and Messner in 1999. Veysey and Messner (1999) concluded, similarly to Sampson and Groves, that variables related to social disorganization partially mediated the effect of structural characteristics on community victimization rate. They also found that unsupervised peer groups had the largest effect on the outcome measures. Lowenkamp et al. were able to replicate the Veysey and Messner analysis using variables and measures similar to those used by Sampson and Groves.

8

Social Disorganization and Strain Theories: A Historical Perspective on Contemporary Theories of Criminology

Their findings were supportive of the major social disorganization theory with few exceptions addressed herein.

A Brief Overview of the "Chicago School," Ecological Theory, & Social Disorganization

Social disorganization theory draws a nexus between crime rates and characteristics that are ecological (based upon the environment) in nature. Sampson opines criminal behavior was influenced by the environment in which an individual lives (Sampson & Groves, 1989). This theory attributes the inadequacy of social controls in addressing various forms of delinquent behavior. Thus, subsequent to the earlier social disorganization theories, social controls become a focus, which impacts criminal behavior effects. Examples of the lack of social controls include inadequate or incomplete teaching of socialization skills taught by family, weak institutions such as church and police, and the detrimental effect of youth maturing in unstable environments, such as broken homes (Sampson & Groves, 1989).

According to Sampson and Groves, the lack of strong support institutions, including churches, businesses, group networks, schools, and police, to youth in environments where social ties are already in-cohesive or weak, creates an absence of reaffirming societal norms and acceptable behavior (Sampson & Groves, 1989). Pursuant to this theory, unstable communities lack infrastructure necessary to deter criminal activity, particularly in residential urban areas. Thus, the lack of steadfast and resolute family and institutional support systems in certain poor communities makes it more likely youth will join in gang activity. Accordingly, this fosters a variety of criminal activities. Sampson concludes that the relevance of structural elements of social disorganization for explaining macro level deviations in violence is supported by empirical data (Sampson & Groves, 1989). This theory has its roots in an analysis of relationships between

Social Disorganization and Strain Theories: A Historical Perspective on Contemporary Theories of Criminology

organisms and their environment. This theory facilitates an understanding of deviant behavior by including empirical data and causation between the environment and individual behavior.

In an article by Lowenkamp, Cullen, and Pratt (2003), the value attributable to systematic replication is recognized. It is noteworthy that Sampson and Groves's original study was built on Shaw and McKay's original models of social disorganization. In 1989, Sampson and Groves extended the model to include additional variables such as urbanization and family disruption. The measures utilized by Sampson and Groves in 1989 in replication studies now include measuring local friendship networks, organizational participation, and unsupervised peer groups. Thus, it is clear the principles of social disorganization theory have been expanded by contemporary theorists such as Sampson and Groves. In replicated studies, only the issue of the mediating effects of social disorganization offered less support for the social disorganization paradigm. Furthermore, only the effect of urbanization was significantly different from 1982 to 1994, using the British study data.

In conclusion, the analysis by Lowenkamp, Cullen, and Pratt (2003) in their commentary on Sampson and Groves' work is supported by a significant quantity of observational data in support of the social disorganization perspective. In addition, the authors concluded their results were consistent with those from Sampson and Groves; however, not all of the relationships that were revealed by Sampson and Groves were exactly replicated using the 1994. This ultimately posits the social disorganization theory is still evolving, i.e., utilizing collective efficacy in different ways than previous studies because it can include core elements of the social disorganization theory and include informal social control in its measures.

Social Disorganization and Strain Theories: A Historical Perspective on Contemporary Theories
of Criminology

Sociologists Shaw and McKay go far beyond previous applications of earlier social
disorganization theorists in defining Social Disorganization Theory and Cultural Transmission
Theory. In their work, *Juvenile Delinquency and Urban Areas* (1942), they examine
repercussions where community institutions cannot match up to a society's norms and the
problems of its residents. These sociologists applied Sutherland's theory of systematic, criminal
behavior (Burgess & Akers, 1966).

Edwin Sutherland, typically known as the originator of differential association theory, was
originally influenced by the Chicago School. School stressed human behavior was influenced by
the environment and other social factors (Tittle, 1986). According to Sutherland, a person is
influenced to become a deviant through association when definitions that are favorable to
aberration are more commonly presented to the individual than negative definitions of law
violation. Sutherland employed the theory of social disorganization in order to help articulate
various increases in criminal behavior, which, together with changes in society, became
particularly abundant in peasant communities. In these communities, variables impacted an
individual were noted to be uniform and consistent. These beliefs led Shaw and McKay to claim
deviant behavior was a normal reaction to abnormal conditions (1942). Nonetheless, there are a
number of weaknesses in Shaw and McKay's work that can now be addressed.

According to Sutherland, criminal behavior is learned in interaction with other deviant
persons. Through this association, specific rationale, and motives are learned. These associations
vary in frequency and duration. Differential association theory attempts to answer the question as
to why people engage in deviant/criminal behavior.

Social Disorganization and Strain Theories: A Historical Perspective on Contemporary Theories of Criminology

As defined, social disorganization fails to adequately address how important ethnic and cultural factors are as they relate to delinquency. It is noteworthy that some criminologists have posited certain individual ethnic groups foster deviant behavior because particular ethnicities may not consider certain deviant behaviors to be inherently wrong or criminal. While the authors state that the conclusion that criminal behaviors are most prevalent in economically depressed or socially undesirable populations is supported by research from various countries (Shaw & McKay, 1942), they do not answer the query as to why a large amount of non-deviant behavior exists in areas that show a high degree of delinquency. One response to this question may be that if a neighborhood has inadequate or weak institutions, there are those individuals who will simply act on their visceral desires and commit crime. The authors acknowledge that rates were frequently assessed employing dependent variables. These variables attempted to measure delinquent activity vis-a-vis arrest records. Various dependent variables in deviant behaviors deemed criminal may be attributable to decisions from courts or the number of arrests. The employment of tools geared toward using dependent variables is yet another example of how social organization has evolved.

In yet another scholarly work, Kurbin and Weitzer (2003) addressed certain factors that have led some to believe there is a need to alter or expand the social disorganization theory. Social disorganization theory employs the power of certain variables used to "mediate the relationship between exogenous structural conditions and neighborhood crime" (Kubrin & Weitzer, 2003). Using various models, such as the dynamic model, analyzing certain relationships under reciprocal and/or contextual effects on individual outcomes would address various interactions, according to Kurbin and Weitzer. Traditionally, social organization theorists

Social Disorganization and Strain Theories: A Historical Perspective on Contemporary Theories of Criminology

fail to examine the relationship between social ties and social control, which are customarily tested as separate mediation variables. Kurbin and Weitzer cite the study performed by Morenoff, Sampson, and Raudenbush (2001), in which it was concluded that homicide in Chicago neighborhoods is impacted by collective efficacy and disadvantage. Furthermore, social networks only impacted homicide through the promotion of residential capacity to achieve social control and unity (Morenoff, 2001).

Kurbin and Weitzer (2003) believe conceptual and methodological reconsideration may be necessary because social ties may take a variety of forms and thus affect the capacity for informal control. The notion of "collective efficacy," portraying the effects of disorder as increasing the fear of crime and crime as reducing informal social control, suggests all measures should be part of a research design so the effects of social relationships, economics, and efficiency can be correlated and compared. This leads to a reconsideration of the significance of cultural influences that were downplayed in analyzing the relationship between crime and ecological concerns under traditional social disorganization theory. Because neighborhoods are culturally and morally diverse, improved models can address these distinctions. Furthermore, social disorganization theory emphasizes informal control over an examination of formal control, which may impact crime and disorder, as well as influence residents' informal control practices.

One example of this emphasis can be examined by researching the effect of police activity in affluent and poor communities. The effect of police activity in neighborhoods where aggressive law enforcement exists suggests police presence is strongest for residents of highly disadvantaged neighborhoods, but weaker in more affluent neighborhoods. The conclusion is deterrence to crime may be affected because potential offenders will risk apprehension if they

Social Disorganization and Strain Theories: A Historical Perspective on Contemporary Theories of Criminology

commit a crime. This suggests restraints are weak. Previous studies neglected to include the effect

of police activity as a variable. This may have led Cohen to reexamine Sutherland's theory

in his work, *Delinquent boys: The culture of the gang* (Cohen, 1955).

Perspectives

Cohen opined that within the lower class, social control was deficient, and a subculture of

delinquency was found. For example, Cohen posited delinquent subcultures are more frequently

located among working class environments. He also criticized the social disorganization theory by

affirming social organization appeared not to account for explaining the origins of

diminishing deviant criminal behavior, nor does the theory facilitate particular delinquent

subcultures. This makes it clear weaknesses in the social organizational theory remain unaddressed

and suggests a defect in assuming social disorganization theory helps to explain deviant criminal

behavior. Cohen posited crime culture is present in various social groups, such as gangs, and by

virtue of participation, people acquire values based upon deviant behaviors

(Cohen, 1955).

Cohen tried to determine the reason why delinquency was more dominant in lower income

groups. Cohen's argument is known as the culture conflict theory, and resembles Sutherland's.

Cohen's theory states that respective institutions or a particular society will operate in order that

each person or group will increase the benefits that improve cultural changes. (Cohen, 1958; also

see Tooby, 1992). Furthermore, Cohen's theory helps to explain political theories of communism

and socialism by diminishing the significance of functionalism; this stresses the influence on

society of how various institutions function. Cohen has articulated one reason for the rejection of

the middle class by delinquent under-classes; middle-class ethics are

Social Disorganization and Strain Theories: A Historical Perspective on Contemporary Theories of Criminology

foreign to the standards under which delinquent boys are raised. To Cohen's credit, criticism of culture conflict theory is still called for, as theory is woefully inadequate in explaining different definitions of morality that foster delinquency in areas not classified as middle class. It is blatantly clear that the most important theory that influenced Cohen was and remains Merton's strain theory. This dictates analysis of control theory and differential association theory (Cohen, 1955).

An examination of Matsueda's control theory and the differential association theory is the subject of Costello and Vowell's (1999) article. Matsueda's study ultimately concluded adopting Sutherland's theory stands for the proposition that differential association theory mediates the effect of social control measures of social bonds and friends' delinquency. In contrast to Matsueda's findings, Costello and Vowell concluded that peer delinquency and social bonds have important impacts on delinquency, and to a greater effect than Matsueda's utilization of definitions (1999).

Costello and Vowell identify noteworthy problems within the study that affected Matsueda's conclusions. Some of these problems include Matsueda's exclusion of females from samples and his use of cross-sectional data. Accordingly, Matsueda's revelations are incomplete because his study does not include many crucial constructs, an example of which is Hirschi's theory, based in part on the principle that all elements of the social bond have direct effects on delinquency. In addition, Matsueda used background variables not usually associated with the control theory perspective.

In Costello and Vowell's article (1999), they highlight that Matsueda's omission of commitment to long term goals is a serious problem given that they found this commitment acts

Social Disorganization and Strain Theories: A Historical Perspective on Contemporary Theories of Criminology

as a preventative measure to delinquency. Costello and Vowell also take issue with Matsueda's definitions prior to delinquency; they indicate that the central difference between the models is whether variables have a direct effect versus an indirect effect through definitions on delinquency. It is also noteworthy that Matsueda utilized only one of Hirschi's measures of attachment to parents and he did not explain the effects of four background variables on delinquency from a control theory perspective.

Costello and Vowell also conclude the social bond is a more important predictor of delinquency than are "definitions" or friends' delinquency as proffered by Matsueda (Costello & Vowell, 1999). Ultimately, these authors have rightfully concluded the specifications derived from control theory must include such items as whether belief influences an individual's choice of delinquent or non-delinquent friends. Matsueda failed to address how the social control theory is at least as plausible as the differential theory. The call by Costello and Vowell for additional theoretical development and careful model specifications that closely correspond with existing theoretical statements (as a result of their reanalysis) is valuable if a critical evaluation of Matsueda's work is a primary goal in furthering the examination of social disorganization theory.

Costello and Vowell establish that social bond elements have a great influence on the selection of friends (Costello & Vowell, 1999). This supports the notion is not explained by differential association theory. Social control theory addresses self-selection of friends and why social bonds and friends' delinquency have direct effects on one's own delinquency. This finding contradicts Matsueda's claim that definitions have stronger direct effects on delinquency than social bonds and friends' delinquency, and allows Costello and Vowell to conclude control theory provides a better explanation of delinquency than differential association theory. Social

Social Disorganization and Strain Theories: A Historical Perspective on Contemporary Theories of Criminology

control theory is more responsive to the question as to why people obey or break rules of society. This theory emphasizes the notion people either commit or obey criminal laws because of weaknesses of the forces that restrain them. Social control adherents also believe that the consequences of violent acts are heightened by social controls, including arrest, incarceration, and loss of earnings (Costello & Vowell, 1999).

The importance of Sutherland's theory is also worth noting. He believed that an individual does not invent illegal conduct if he has not been taught crime. Differential association is another criminological theory attributable to Sutherland. He was of the belief that when we interact with other individuals we learn about the motives fostering or attributable to deviant behavior deemed criminal. Sutherland focuses on how individuals learn how to actually engage in illegal/criminal behavior. Sutherland does not address in his studies why individuals become criminals. As these individuals continue to engage in crimes, according to Sutherland, they also learn attitudes, rationalizations, and motives. According to Sutherland, individuals find it easier to commit crimes. Sutherland suggests criminal behavior is learned; the essential element when learning objectively about deviant criminal activity is to understand the complex nature of motivation, values, attitudes, as well as the subjective subclass's acceptability of middle class morality and respect for the law. One of the weaknesses often cited of Sutherland's theory is the lack of empirical data in testing the fundamental principles, as noted by Pratt et al. (2012). The argument is made that criminological theory students have not quickly engaged in the task of reviewing contemporary perspectives methodically and thoroughly, particularly through the use of meta-analytic techniques aimed at synthesizing amassed knowledge (Pratt et al., 2012).

ial Disorganization and Strain Theories: A Historical Perspective on Contemporary
eories of Criminology

In contrast to Sutherland's differential association theory, sociologist Akers, a known

vocate of social learning theory, suggests Sutherland's perspectives are actually enhanced by

cial learning theory (Akers, Krohn, & Kaduce, 1979). However, Akers also suggests that

finitions can be either general or specific; that is, they may broadly approve or disapprove of

ne, or they may be situation specific (Akers et al., 1979). Thus, influences such as "imitation"

d analyzing acts that are reinforced by reward or avoidance of discomfort, must be addressed.

While narrative reviews have favorably concluded social control theory and its foundation

differential association behavior give this theory some credence, it is equally true many

nificant issues still exist, even though it has a strong foundation in empirical data. The use of

ta-analysis by Pratt et al. (2012) concluded the differential association predictors were robust;

wever, large differences were found in mean effect sizes of the impact of differential association

iables and crime. These effect sizes ranged from weak prediction by others' attitudes to robust

diction by peers' behaviors. The authors conclude that further empirical evaluation is critical

reaching more definitive conclusions about crime. Thus, advocates of social learning theory

ss the inclusion of empirical attention in testing a variety of predictors and variables that may

xcluded in other theories. Social learning theory attempts to explain deviance by integrating

iables with encouraged delinquency, with other variables that discourage delinquency.

The Social Learning School

In theory, adopting the principles of the social learning school should prevent future deviant

avior. However, the theory does not seem to address how, from the onset, criminal behavior can

revented. Anderson (1999) narrates a story entitled, "The Decent Daddy." This

Social Disorganization and Strain Theories: A Historical Perspective on Contemporary Theories of Criminology

story is a reflection on urban street violence and those individuals who play a significant part in whether or not youths turn to delinquent behavior or are impacted positively by affirmative social values (church, family, school). The narrative is yet another attempt to explain criminal deviant behavior through the use of a narrative. The failure to utilize the narrative by social disorganization theorists is yet another impact that earlier criminologists failed to address and would not have come to light but for such a failure. Consequently, one can look to the narrative and social learning theory as one of the many tools criminologists can employ when studying criminal behavior.

Anderson (2000) portrays the problem of youth violence and the effect of role models on behavior of a strong black man who is still the embodiment of "grit." Anderson narrates a story about an individual named Martin. He is what Anderson has labeled a "Decent Daddy." In contemporary society, his role as a father is being devastated through the loss of jobs in a society where the talents of a man of color may not be appreciated (Anderson, 2000). The decent daddy's home is described as a "protected nest." (Anderson, 2000, p. The values and morality of this one particular poor black man are acknowledged by other youths in spite of the poverty and street violence; this respected role model can have a significant impact and steer youths away from deviant criminal behavior.

All of this literature has led to the assessment of major deficiencies in Sutherland's differential theory, in particular, the conclusions revealed by Matsueda by failing to address the significance of control theory on outcomes. It is interesting to note the present analysis and examination of social disorganization theory has now led to a further analysis of the various strengths and weaknesses of the control, differential association, and social learning theories.

One of the most significant issues Gottfredson and Hirschi (1990) addressed in their book

...that many theories attempt to explain or analyze crimes and are woefully inadequate

...dressing the actual "nature" of crime. Gottfredson and Hirschi opine that self-control is an

...portant correlate of antisocial behavior, and therefore, the authors have penned a new definition

...crime. Their definition is, "...[crime] is acts of force or fraud undertaken in pursuit of self-

...erest" (p. 15). Accordingly, they seem to argue self-control appears malleable during the first 7-8

...rs of life, but after this point, while self-control tends to improve with age as socialization

...tinues to occur, it is largely unresponsive to any intervention effort. In regards to self-control,

...tfredson and Hirschi believe that individual differences are formed in early life and remain

...ly stable across time (p. 77). Thus, self-control is not deterministic. This conclusion implies

...formal criminal justice system can play only a minor role in the prevention and control

...crime.

Gottfredson and Hirschi (1990) theorize that some individuals will engage in risky

...aviors because they are merely seeking instant gratification (p. 91). This, according to the

...ors, is attributable in part to low self-control. Therefore, according to Gottfredson and Hirschi,

...laining crime is really quite simple; any age-crime relationship is invariant over time,

...e, and culture, so it is in no need of social explanation. If, as posited, criminal theories have

...ries of the offender at their root, then offender traits are less predictive of crime than

...ronmental and situational factors. This, according to the authors, is attributable to level of self-

...rol. For example, if a young child exhibits aggression or impulsive behavior, the parents are

...able because a child's low self-control is the result of poor parenting, supervision, and

...alization skills. This results in the appealing temptations of crime, i.e., instant gratification.

Social Disorganization and Strain Theories: A Historical Perspective on Contemporary Theories of Criminology

According to Gottfredson and Hirschi, victims of criminal behavior become easy targets because of lack of self-control by the perpetrator, which positively correlates to weak family structure.

A peer of mine who grew up in a highly affluent home, and to all external appearances, was firmly established in a stable, congenial, loving, and nurturing family (what many might categorize as an "all American traditional home"). Both parents exercised strong parenting skills. They were involved in their children's' education, church, and extracurricular activities. The children got along well with their peers and adults. They were respectful and academically successful; however, one child, "John," exhibited changes in his development after reaching the age of twelve. His socialization skills deteriorated; he no longer exhibited high self-control and became a criminal offender. Thus, Gottfredson and Hirschi's proposition "...individual differences in self-control are established early in life and are reasonably stable thereafter," appears to be an anomaly in the example at hand (1990, p. 177).

Not only socialization agents are correlated to potential for criminal behavior. After many years of rehabilitation, the medical and psychiatric evaluations and reports revealed John's envy of other family members' "talents," would not have revealed itself in the early years of his childhood. Not all criminal behavior can be conceptually connected to reckless behavior. Crime and deviant behavior is not as simple as theorized by Gottfredson and Hirschi (1990). One must take into account the characteristics of offenders, and not simply look to spatial and temporal distributions of people or events.

Gottfredson and Hirsch's (1990) book examines the conceptualization of crime, which according to the authors is particularized into six elements of low self-control. Accordingly, acting out a crime is merely a reckless act that individuals with low self-control will participate

Social Disorganization and Strain Theories: A Historical Perspective on Contemporary Theories of Criminology

in because low self-control is a result of lack of discipline. Crime appeals to those with low self-control levels. There exists individuals who exhibit low self-control and cannot delay instant gratification. Other scholars such as Gottfredson and Hirsch (1990) opine that crime requires no skill or perseverance. These authors' also hypothesise that victims of crime experience pain, highlighting the link between self-centeredness and having low levels of self-control.

Ethnicity, race, and culture, according to Gottfredson and Hirschi (1990), affect self-control levels because they have incidental impacts on parental socialization. One critic of Gottfredson and Hirschi's theory of social control was Akers, who opined there is a need for an independent indicator of self-control (1991). Some criminologists believe that some crimes cannot be explained by low self-control, such as white-collar crimes.

Gottfredson and Hirschi (1990) attempt to explain all types of criminal behavior in a general way. There are developmental theories such as those discussed by Moffitt, life course theories as theorized by Sampson and Laub, and other criminological theories that do not appear to be as focused on traditional parenting skills. Traditional parenting skills appears to be a major variable Gottfredson and Hirschi utilize in explaining criminal behavior as the result of low self-control. Thus, social control theory tends to downplay life course theory. While the implication of life course theory is that cultural expectations directly impact the decision made by an individual to commit illegal acts, social control theory implies individuals who engage in crime during adolescent years remain likely to possess the same motivation to commit crimes and deviance throughout life. Furthermore, Gottfredson and Hirschi do not address or explain gender and age effects on differences in crime; however, they do discuss differences in socialization of

Social Disorganization and Strain Theories: A Historical Perspective on Contemporary Theories of Criminology

young children by gender and resulting levels of self-control that are not developed. The authors also do not address the effect of race on criminal activity.

Self-control theories do not properly account for empirical evidence and other variables that have an impact on criminal behavior, recidivism, and delinquency. Self-control theory remains general, and overly simplistic. Gottfredson and Hirschi suggest crime and other risk-taking behaviors can be linked to low self-control at the individual level (1990). The assertion being made is low self-control is a commonality that can be objectively established as a characteristic in all criminals. Other scholars have reveal variables which affect criminal behavior. Thus, corporate criminologists expect organizational characteristics as manifested in the behavior of individuals, not low self-control, explain corporate illegality. On balance, if the theory cannot account for the offending patterns of corporate managers, then one of its main claims as a general theory is challenged.

Another study by Pratt, et.al. (2012) concluded that the evidence thus far is consistent with the theory. Pratt and Cullen (2012) also empirically summarized 21 tests, and found that when self-control is held constant, differential association and delinquent definitions have significant effects on delinquency. It is also notable, however, that not one study reviewed by Pratt and Cullen examined corporate offending. Additionally, to date only three criminological studies have examined the effects of parenting on self-control. A critical analysis of the empirical evidence generated in other studies suggests a number of unresolved issues regarding the self-control theory remain to be investigated. flay (2001) stated there is some support for self-control theory from empirical studies, yet the theory does not provide the conclusive explanation of

Social Disorganization and Strain Theories: A Historical Perspective on Contemporary Theories of Criminology

crime intended by Gottfredson and Hirschi. To simply explain crime and deviance as the consequence of some generic result of easy gratification is less than acceptable.

Hay also conducted research aimed at assessing the expectation of self-control theory regarding parenting effect on juvenile delinquency. He concluded "...self-control theory's conceptualization of effective parenting may be unnecessarily narrow" (Hay, 2001, p. 719). Hay also addressed the deficiency of self-control theory by analyzing whether low self-esteem mediates the effects of parenting on delinquency. One result of his study was that a moderate correlation existed between parental discipline and monitoring. Additionally, when a broader set of variables are used to test self-control theory, the variance explained more than doubles. Hay also declares findings may alter criminological theory by showing self-control in children develops in more varied ways than previously thought.

Empirical Studies

Empirical studies of corporate offending, both qualitative and quantitative, have found a number of intra- and extra-organizational characteristics are associated with offending. Empirical literature focuses mainly on the role organizational structure and culture play in offending (or, conversely, ethical) decisions. Less research attention has been paid to the cultural, competitive, and regulatory environments of firms (Vaughan, 1999). Across studies, the evidence is somewhat inconsistent and the causal mechanisms of offending murky, perhaps because the relative magnitude of factors may vary by offense type or because effects are rarely examined simultaneously. In Simpson and Piquero's (2002) article, the authors concluded that intentions are significantly influenced by nine organizational-level factors, even when accounting for similar behavior. Examining the vignette items, manager's offending intentions were

Social Disorganization and Strain Theories: A Historical Perspective on Contemporary Theories of Criminology

significantly influenced by instrumental concerns. The study concluded that offending increases when the industry is losing ground to foreign competitors, when the illegal act is likely to save the company a large amount of money, and when crime is viewed as a way to change an existing law (Simpson & Piquero, 2002).

In 2004, Pratt, Turner, and Piquero examined low levels of restraint, discriminatory association, and social learning and prepared respective analyses of the impact of poor parenting. Although Gottfredson and Hirschi are often cited for the proposition that self-control alone influences delinquency and criminality, weaknesses in their theory become obvious due to the failure to account for certain cognitive processes that consider the effect of consequences and opportunity. Thus, situational factors can also affect criminal behavior, not merely self-control alone. Based on empirical data and other relevant criticism of the self-control theory, it is unconvincing that self-control, unilaterally, is the best theory in light of empirical evidence tested against the theory.

According to Pratt and Cullen (2000), Gottfredson and Hirschi's view of self-control stems from their perspective on crime. Thus, it would follow Gottfredson and Hirschi's logic that as crime involves little preparation, requires few skills, and is easily gratifying, it is easy to commit. Gottfredson and Hirschi have not bifurcated or distinguished between an understanding of crime and an understanding of criminals; they are not one and the same. This, according to Pratt and Cullen, cultivated a theory known as tautology. (Gottfredson, 2000).

The development of life course criminologists appears to be a reaction to other criminologists that adhere to the self-control theory. The theory posits criminology cannot account for age variations. The antithesis is theorized by life course criminologists, who assert

Social Disorganization and Strain Theories: A Historical Perspective on Contemporary Theories of Criminology

age variations are significant as a variable in determining criminal behavior and deviance. There are those who are still critical of the life course theorists and still maintain social learning theories actually do account for age variations and patterns of behavior over the life time of an individual. The arguments made by Moffitt (1993) address delinquency. He argues that there are separate and unique categories of individuals, each with their own etiologies, He also opines that more extensive quantitatively extensive groups also expose anti-social behavior. Moffitt asserts a number of poignant concluions. First he posits that anti social conduct will always exist in some groups of anti social personalities.Subsequently, Moffit opines thatvarious examinations contain chains that initiate in early life. Finally Moffitt believes that some behaviors are related to neurological predispositions and there are at least two categories which explain consistent deviant and criminal sociopathic behaviors. (Moffitt, 1993).

These two types of interaction are described by Moffitt as reactive interaction and proactive interaction. Moffitt views life course persistent antisocial behavior as normative rather than abnormal. This supports a theory that posits adolescent onset delinquency is the equivalent to social mimicry of a pathological type of anti-social child. Thus, Moffitt concludes that etiology of consistent anti-social behavior will reveal more results if studies originate with prenatal behavior and follow the individual to adulthood. Moffitt is critical of those criminologists who do not follow adolescents to adulthood.

McGloin, Pratt, and Piquero (2006) reveal inadequacies in prior studies that concluded Maternal Cigarette Smoking (MCS) is a proxy for psychological deficit rather than a precursor. They studied the link between MCS and crime/deviance, and concluded criminological research has used MCS as a proxy. They showed the CAT (California Achievement Test) was a

Social Disorganization and Strain Theories: A Historical Perspective on Contemporary Theories of Criminology

significant tool to address the potential conceptual, empirical, and ideological concerns with using the IQ to assess neuropsychological functioning. Thus, neuropsychological deficit did not appear to mediate the relationship between MCS and Life-Course Persistent (LCP) offending. The authors further illustrate the need for two primary potential mediators that should be addressed in future research. These included parenting and how MCS is a known risk factor for temperamental and conduct problems. They also note there may be a genetic variable of interest as well, e.g., inherited dispositions.

Pratt, McGloin, and Fearn (2006) addressed MCS and its' effects during pregnancy on criminal/deviant behavior. The focus of this article was whether or not there is a substantively meaningful association between MCS and criminal/deviant behavior. The authors concluded that neuropsychological deficit and self-control need not be mutually exclusive explanations of the MCS-crime relationship. After analyzing and observing empirical data, the authors note MCS is in fact a moderately important factor for criminal/deviant behavior. However, significantly, they also note there are other individually associated characteristics that are more strongly associated with deviant behavior, such as self-control and antisocial attitudes. This is not to say that maternal cigarette smoking during pregnancy has no effect on criminal/deviant behavior, but rather that there are more proximal predictors of crime/deviance that do and should receive the lion's share of criminologists' attention.

Contemporary Criminologists

Cullen, Gendreau, Jarjoura, and Wright (1997) wrote a rather scathing commentary on the woeful inadequacies and biases contained in Herrnstein and Murray's, *The Bell Curve: Intelligence and Class Structure in American Life*. Their claim is that Murray's message is

Social Disorganization and Strain Theories: A Historical Perspective on Contemporary Theories of Criminology

misleading and erroneous. Furthermore they believe Murray et al., have employed a narrow, outdated conceptualization of intelligence, for claiming IQ is difficult to boost, and for implying African-Americans are intellectually inferior (as cited in Gould, 1984, p. 388). It appears rather clear from a myriad of criminologists that IQ is in fact a risk factor in juvenile and adult crime (Cullen, et. al. 1997). However, as Cullen and his peers have noted, the magnitude of the effect of IQ on criminal behavior is the vital issue. Cullen has pointed to empirical data, which examined the impact of IQ on system processing, interviewing and penetration into the criminal justice system, which seems to suggest Hermstein and Murray's analysis of IQ and delinquent/crime are misleading since their conclusions were not based on scientific evidence, but on, perhaps, on broad assumptions. Cullen and his peers have illustrated IQ is at best a modest predictor of crime; many other factors are much stronger criminological risk factors. Cullen has also noted there is an emerging movement in psychology to broaden the conceptualization of IQ to include practical intelligence, something not addressed by Hermstein or Murray. Thus Cullen and his co-authors conclude Hermstein and Murray who are cited by Arthur S Goldberger and Charles F. Manski (1995) are cognitively challenged criminologists.

In 2004, McGloin, Pratt, and Maahs, addressed the concept that criminologists treated the relationship between IQ and delinquency as direct, linear, and casual. These cited authors' stressed the hypotheses of Farrington, Jolliffe, Loeber, Stouthammer-Loeber & Kalb (2001) that ignores such variables as how IQ has an indirect influence on school performance and how deviant peer relationships may also effect IQ and its relationship with delinquency. Therefore, they assert there are many indirect pathways for the IQ delinquency link that cannot be evaluated based upon middle class measuring rod theories. McGloin and co-authors poignantly illustrate

Social Disorganization and Strain Theories: A Historical Perspective on Contemporary Theories of Criminology

that integrating the concept of self-control into the present framework is also important given

Gottfredson and Hirschi's discussion of the potential criminogenic effects of poor school

performance and deviant peer associations. The authors conclude that a variety of variables

affecting IQ and intelligence and empirical evidence suggesting a relationships between IQ and

deviant behavior have been overlooked. Thus, elements of social bond/social control, deviant peer

pressure, and empirically defensible explanations of the 1Q-delinquency relationship are plausible.

McGloin, Sullivan, Piquero, and Pratt (2007) revealed frequently overlooked variables that

suggest various changes in life circumstances may impact criminal behavior. These authors have,

in a somewhat novel way, researched the extent to which certain events bear upon shifting pockets

of offending specialization over time. The focus of their article appears to be why certain changes

in life events also lead offenders to specialize in particular crimes. The focus of research by

McGloin et al. is not quantitative, but rather a search for explanations as to why certain offenders

become specialized, at least in the short term. Pratt and Cullen (2012) have posited self-control,

may be one trait characteristic where individual's behavior exists along a "continuum" (McGloin,

2007, p. 325). The authors suggest that changes in illegal opportunities, such as marriage and

drinking, may be related to offending. Propensity theorists conclude relationships between these

events and offending specialization are spurious due to the endogenous nature of criminal

propensity measures (Pratt et al., 2012). There are also those theorists who focus on the relative

validity of opportunity to explain offending specialization. As the authors aptly point out, these

scholars are not necessarily in conflict with each other. They may not be independent of each other.

This notion is stressed in the data evaluation conducted in

Social Disorganization and Strain Theories: A Historical Perspective on Contemporary Theories of Criminology

study of male offenders incarcerated in Nebraska from 1989 to 1990 (Homey & Marshall, 2006). They utilized a diversity index in this study along with various independent variables called local life circumstances, or LLCs) as well as offending frequencies, which propensity theorists posit has a mediating effect on the prediction of offending specialization from LLCs. The study reveals from the data and variables utilized that short term changes in LLCs matter. The results also suggest increases in LLCs in regards to drug and alcohol use likely lead to increased criminal variation. In addition, the results of this study imply that LLCs are not only related to short term forms of criminal activity committed, but also prevalence of offences.

Finally, the authors suggest both propensity and opportunity models for offending/specialization do not have to be viewed as competing theories. Thus, qualitative shifts in criminal offending are related to LLCs and may even have a nexus with offenses across gender (Homey & Marshall, 2006). This article addressed certain social events occur in an individual's life may actually increase offending specialization. This was never addressed by social disorganization theorists and remains a weakness to be reexamined. Reading through this article and ideas for future research on LLCs was most informative since it addressed the notion that both propensity theorists and those theorists who focus on opportunity, can coexist and help explain offending/specialization.

Application by Contemporary Theorists

Cohen and Felson's (1979) article proved somewhat archaic and provincial in that it appeared to suggest a routine activity methodology explains the paradox of increasing criminal activity. These may be attributable to changes in the labor force, as well as single adult households subsequent to the end of the Second World War. These authors view the

Social Disorganization and Strain Theories: A Historical Perspective on Contemporary Theories of Criminology

interdependence between offenders and victims as a predatory relationship (Cohen & Felson, 1979). They also attribute the increase in crime rates to levels of technology. The theory is problematic as it tends to emphasize and focus on family activities as a panacea for lowering rates of criminal victimization and the eagerness by some to commit crimes because of the quantity and emphasis on durable goods in an ever-growing technologically promoted society. The significant deficits in this approach are rather obvious. Unlike the discussions and reports revealed from the LLC studies, Cohen and Felson overemphasize the significance of various household indicators and seemingly treat LLCs with benign neglect. To attribute a lack of social control and increased crime to the deficiencies in the criminal justice system in exerting social control is a leap of faith. For these reasons noted above, this particular article was less informative and certainly less persuasive than Pratt and Cullen or McGloin and his co-authors in the first enumerated article. Although all of the readings proved somewhat informative, Pratt and Cullen's (2005) article suggested many criminologists focus predominantly on why certain individuals break the law. These scholars often also focus on "risk factors" in order to cultivate theories of criminality. Pratt and Cullen, described in great detail meta-analysis, the deficiencies in narrative reviews because they are qualitative, and utilizing meta-analysis as an alternative approach integrates multiple independent tests in a more objective manner than in traditional approaches where observation and empirical data are the units of analysis. My position is hat there are many advantages to meta-analysis, including but not limited to the precise estimates of effect size, methodological variations, public coding decisions, and having a dynamic database. Unlike Shaw and McKay who focused on the the social disorganization theory, Pratt and Cullen also examined characteristics that foster criminal activity in high crime neighborhoods compared to

Social Disorganization and Strain Theories: A Historical Perspective on Contemporary Theories of Criminology

low crime neighborhoods. Their study tends to support the discussion proffered by McGloin, et al., as an example, the empirical status of resource/economic deprivation theory as favorable. Therefore, poverty, and other LLCs in an individual's life would have a correlation or nexus in explaining offending/specialization not simply "risk factors."

Some prior studies, such as conducted by Farrington in 2002, concluded offending increased to age 17 and then declined. (Farrington, 2002). Sampson and Laub opine persistent offenders can be defined by certain objective variables such as arrest frequency, incarceration time, and arrests in each decade. Laub and Sampson offer some alternatives to these approaches, however. Firstly, they state that "a life course framework focuses on the historical time and place recognizes lives are embedded and shaped by context; developmental impact of live events is contingent on when these events occur" (Sampson & Laub, 2003, p.478). They go on to indicate the significant impact of interdependency and personal agency on construction of a life course framework. The authors approach appears to be compatible with social control, social learning and rational choice theories. However, the approach proffered by Sampson and Laub takes into account contingencies and the role of chance and they have modified the social control theory to take into consideration these variables. The authors take into account various person based narratives to explain and analyze the processes of desistance and persistence in crime. They accomplish this by exploring such institutions as marriage, and work, which impact desistance from crime and how even military service may present unique opportunities for the poor or disadvantaged by asserting positive influences on prior adverse influences.

Social Disorganization and Strain Theories: A Historical Perspective on Contemporary Theories of Criminology

The narratives and firsthand accounts explore various processes such as agency in situational arenas. These narratives frequently encapsulate through life experiences the personal-situational context and historical context of certain events during the life course of events and thus, provide insight, formerly treated with benign or outright neglect in previous studies of social control theory. Sampson and Laub have discerned why their modified approach integrating quantitative and qualitative data, in their attempt to understand persistent and desistance from crime over the life course, may be the best approach.

Conclusion and Call for Research

Social disorganization and theory evolved significantly over time. Many of the subsequent theories cultivated by contemporary criminologists cite these two theories as one of a number of causative factors in explaining criminal behavior while adding their own respective examinations and studies ultimately lead them to new hypothesis. Critical thinking and analysis would dictate the need for continued research may lead to less bias or skewed results and greater objectivity in response to a myriad of questions criminologists wish to answer.

The developments by contemporary scholars should continue to address deficiencies in prior theoretical models such as earlier strain and social disorganization theories proffered by earlier criminologists. This remains a challenge to the academic who desires to find the panacea or singular explanation for deviance in society. This is a monumental task for followers of a specific or unique school of thought. Consequently, a new model or paradigm should be created by those seeking answers that neither dismisses nor unilaterally accepts prior critical thought and study is the product of the scientific method.

Social Disorganization and Strain Theories: A Historical Perspective on Contemporary Theories of Criminology

References

Acker, J. R., Bohm, **R. M.,** & Lanier, C. S. (Eds.), America's experiment with capital punishment: Reflections on the past, present, and future of the ultimate penal sanction (2nd ed.). Durham, NC: Carolina Academic Press.

Agnew, R. (1992). Foundation for a general strain theory of crime and delinquency. *Criminology, 30(1),* 47-87.

Anderson, E. (2000). *Code of the street: Decency, violence, and the moral life of the inner city.* Chicago, Illinois. University of Chicago Press.

Akers, R. L., Krohn, M. D., Lanza-Kaduce, L., & Radosevich, M. (1979). Social learning and deviant behavior: A specific test of a general theory. *American Sociological Review, 44,* 635-655.

Blackburn, A., Mullings, J., & Marquart, J. (2008). Sexual assault in prison and beyond: Toward an understanding of lifetime sexual assault among incarcerated women. *The Prison Journal, 88(3),* 351-377.

Burgess, R. L., & Akers, R. L. (1966). A differential association-reinforcement theory of criminal behavior. *Social Problems,14,* 228-247.

Cohen, A. K. (1955). *Delinquent boys: The culture of the gang.* Mankato, Minnesota: The Free Press.

Cohen, A., & Short, J. (1958). Research in delinquent subcultures. *Journal of Social Issues,* 14 (3) 20-37.

Cohen, L. E., & Felson, M. (1979). Social change and crime rate trends: A routine activity approach. *American Sociological Review,* 44(4), 588-608.

Social Disorganization and Strain Theories: A Historical Perspective on Contemporary
Theories of Criminology

Costello, B. J., & Vowell, P. R. (1999). Testing control theory and differential association: A
    reanalysis of the Richmond youth project data. *Criminology 37*, 815-842.

Cullen, F. T., Gendreau, P., Jarjoura, G. R., & Wright, J. P. (1997). Crime and the bell curve:
    Lessons from intelligent criminology. *Crime & Delinquency, 43(4),* 387-441.

Cullen, F. T., Wright, J. P., & Blevins, K. R. (2009). *Taking stock: The status of criminological
    theory.* New York, New York: Transaction Publishers.

Dailey, P. (2002). Policy implications relating to inmate mothers and their children: Will
    the past be prologue? *The Prison Journal, 82(2),* 234-268.

Durkheim, E. (1982). *The rules of sociological method.* New York, New York: Simon and
    Schuster.

Eigenberg, H. (2000). Correctional officers and their perceptions of homosexuality, rape, and
    prostitution in male prisoners. *The Prison Journal, 80(4),* 415-433.

Fairhurst, L. (n.d.). FSU study: Parents may have longer to influence kids' self-control. Retrieved
    from http://fsu.edu/news/2006/11/27/criminology.study

Farrington, D. P. d. Jolliffe, D., Loeber, R. Stouthmmer-Loeber, M. & Kalb, L. (2001). The
    Concentration of offenders in families, and family criminality in the prediction of boys'
    delinquency. *Journal o fAdolescents, 24,* 579-596.

Fradella, H. (2003). Faith, delusions, and death. *Journal of Contemporary Criminal Justice,
    19(1),* 98-113.

Gillis v. Litscher, 468 F.3d 488, 493 (7th Cir.2006).
Goldberger, A., & Manski, C. (1995). Review Article: The Bell Curve by Herrnstein and Murray.
    Journal of Economic Literature. 33(2), 762-766.

Social Disorganization and Strain Theories: A Historical Perspective on Contemporary Theories of Criminology

Gottfredson, M., & Hirschi, T. (1990). *A general theory of crime.* Stanford, CA: Stanford
    University Press.

Gould, S. J. (1984). Human equality is a contingent fact of history. *Natural History, 93,* 26-33.

    Greek, C (1999). Survey of Criminological Theory (Spring). Retrieved from
    https://www.criminology.fsu.edu/crimtheory/cohen.htm

Hay, C. (2001). Parenting, self-control, and delinquency: A test of self-control theory.
    Criminology, 39(3), 707-736.

Homey, J., & Marshall, I. (2006) Risk perceptions among serious offenders: The role of crime
    and punishment. *Criminology,* 33, 575-579.

Hunter, G. (2012, December 5). Sexual abuse by prison and jail staff proves persistent. *Pandemic
    Prison Legal News.* Retrieved from https://www.prisonlegalnews.org/default.aspx.

Johnson, R., & McGunigall-Smith, S. (2008). Life without parole: America's other death
            penalty. *The Prison Journal, 88(2),* 328-346.

Johnson, R. (1996). *Hard time: Understanding understanding and reforming the prison* (2nd ed.)
    Belmont, California: Wadsworth Publishing Co.

Kubrin, C. E., & Weitzer, R. (2003). Social disorganization theory. *Journal of Research in Crime
    and Delinquency, 40(4).* 374-402.

Laub, J. H., & Sampson, R. J. (1991). The Sutherland-Glueck debate: On the sociology of
    criminological knowledge. *American Journal of Sociology,* 96, 1402-1440.

Lord, E. (2008). The challenges of mentally ill female offenders in prison. *Criminal
    Justice & Behavior, 35(8),* 928-942.

Social Disorganization and Strain Theories: A Historical Perspective on Contemporary
Theories of Criminology

Lowenkamp, C. T., Cullen, F. T., & Pratt, T. C. (2003). Replicating Sampson and Groves's test of
        social disorganization theory: Revisiting a criminological classic. *Journal of Research in*
        Crime and Delinquency, 40, 351-373.

Marquart, J. (1986) Prison guards and the use of physical coercion as a mechanism of prisoner
        control. *Criminology, 24(2),* 347-366.

Man, C. & Cronan, J. (2001) Forecasting sexual abuse in prison: The prison subculture of
        masculinity as a backdrop for "deliberate indifference." *The Journal of Criminal Law and*
        Criminology, 92, 127-185.

Matsueda, R. L., & Heimer, K. (2009) Race, family structure, and delinquency: A test of
        differential association and social control theories. *American Sociological Review, 52(6),*
        826-840.

McGloin, J. M., Pratt, T. C., & Maahs, J. (2004). Rethinking the IQ-delinquency relationship: A
        longitudinal analysis of multiple theoretical models. *Justice Quarterly, 21(3),* 603-631.

McGloin, J. M., Pratt, T. C., & Piquero, A. R. (2006). A life-course analysis of the criminogenic
        effects of maternal cigarette smoking during pregnancy: A research note on the mediating
        impact of neuropsychological deficit. *Journal of Research in Crime and Delinquency,* 43(4),
        412-426.

Merton, J Kurbin & Weitzer (2009). Macro-Micro Theoetical Integration: An Unexplored
        Theroetical Frontier. *Journal of Theoretical and Philosophical Criminology,* 1, (2),
        33-71.

Merton, R.K. (1938). Social structure and anomie. *American Sociological Review, 3(5),* 672-682.

Merton, R. K. (1968). *Social theory and social structure.* New York: Free Press.

Social Disorganization and Strain Theories: A Historical Perspective on Contemporary
Theories of Criminology

Messner, S.F., Rosenfeld, R. (1997). Political restraint of the market and levels of criminal
    homicide : A cross-national application of Institutional-anomie theory. *Social Forces*,
    75(4), 13-93.

Moffitt, T. E. (1993). Adolescence-limited and life-course-persistent antisocial behavior: A
    developmental taxonomy. *Psychological Review, 100(4)*, 674-701.

Morenoff, J. D., Sampson, R. J., & Raudenbush, S.W. (2001). Neighborhood inequality,
    collective efficacy, and the spatial dynamics of urban violence. *Criminology, 39*, 517-
    558.

National Prison Rape Elimination Act Commission Executive Report. (June 2009). Retrieved
    from: http://www.asca.net/projects/16/pages/161

Opp, K. D. (1979). Social evolution: Learning theory applied to group action. *Theory and
    Decision, 10*, 229-343.

Perez, A., Leifman, S. & Estrada, A. (2003). Reversing the criminalization of mental illness.
    Crime & Delinquency, 49(1), 62-78.

Petersilia, J. (2004). What works in prison reentry? Reviewing and questioning the evidence.
    Federal Probation, 68, 4-8.

Pipher, M. (1995). *Reviving ophelia, saving the selves of adolescent girls*. New York, New York:
    Ballantine Books.

Pogrebin, M.R. & Poole, E.D. (1998). Sex, gender, and work: The case of women jail officers.
    Sociology of Crime, Law, and Deviance, 1, 105-124.

Pratt, T. C., Cullen, F. T., Sellers, C. (2012). The empirical status of social learning theory: A
    meta-analysis. *Justice Quarterly, 27(6)*, 765-802.

Social Disorganization and Strain Theories: A Historical Perspective on Contemporary Theories of Criminology

Pratt, T. C., & Godsey, T. W. (2003). Social support, inequality, and homicide: A cross-national test of an integrated theoretical model. *Criminology, 41,* 611-644.

Pratt, T. C., McGloin, J. M., & Fearn, N. E. (2006). Maternal cigarette smoking during pregnancy and criminal/deviant behavior: A meta-analysis. *International Journal of Offender Therapy and Comparative Criminology 50(6),* 672-690.

Pratt, T. C., Turner, M. G., & Piquero, A. R. (2004). Parental socialization and community context: A longitudinal analysis of the structural sources of low self-control. *Journal of Research in Crime and Delinquency,* 41(3), 219-243.

Sampson, R., & Groves, W. B. (1989) Community structure and crime: Testing social disorganization theory. *American Journal of Sociology, 94,* 774-802.

Sampson, R. J., & Laub, J. H. (1993). *Crime in the making: Pathways and turning points through life.* Cambridge, MA: Harvard University Press.

Shaw, C. R., & McKay, H. D. (1942). *Juvenile delinquency and urban areas.* Chicago: University of Chicago Press.

Simpson, S. S., & Piquero, N. L. (2002). Low self-control, organizational theory, and corporate crime. *Law & Society Review,* 36(3), 509-548.

Sutherland, E.. (1961). *White-collar crime.* New York, N.Y. Holt, Rinehart and Winston, Inc

Sutherland., E., (1937). *The professional thief* Chicago: The University of Chicago.

Tooby, J., & Cosmides, L. (1992). The psychological foundations of culture. In A. Editor & B. Editor (Eds.), *The adapted mind: Evolutionary psychology and the generation of culture* New York: Cambridge University Press.

Social Disorganization and Strain Theories: A Historical Perspective on Contemporary Theories of Criminology

Tittle, C. (1998) The Remarkable Persistence of a Flawed Theory:: A Rejoinder to Matsueda
    Theoretical Criminology 2, 85-92.

Unnever, J. D., Cullen, F. T., & Pratt, T. C. (2003). Parental management, ADHD, and delinquent
    involvement. Reassessing Gottfredson and Hirschi's general theory. *Justice Quarterly, 20(3),*
    471-500.

Unnever, J. D., Cullen, F. T., & Pratt, T. C. (n.d.) Why is "Bad" parenting criminogenic? A test of
    rival theories. Retrieved from ttp://www.radford.edutjunnever/artieles/badparenting.pdf

Tewksbury, R., & West, A. (2000). Research on sex in prison during the late 1980s and early
    1990s. *The Prison Journal, 80(4),* 368-378.

Toch, H. (2008). Punitiveness as "behavior management." *Criminal Justice & Behavior, 35(3),*
    388-397.

Vaughan, D. (1999).The dark side of organizations: Mistake, misconduct, and disaster . *Annual
    Review of Sociology, 25,* 271-305.

Veysey, B. M., & Messner, S. F. (1999). Further testing of social disorganization theory: An
    elaboration of Sampson and Groves's 'community structure and crime'. *Journal of
    Research in Crime and Delinquency, 36,* 156-174.

Wyatt v. Stickney,_325 F. Supp 781(M. D. Ala.1971), 334 F. Supp. 1341 (M. D.Ala 1971), 344 F.
    Supp. 373 (M. D. Ala).

www.ingramcontent.com/pod-product-compliance
Lightning Source LLC
Chambersburg PA
CBHW061521180526
45171CB00001B/273